the GREAT WORKPLACE

BUILDING TRUST AND INSPIRING PERFORMANCE

LEADERSHIP Assessment

MICHAEL BURCHELL
AND JENNIFER ROBIN

GREAT PLACE TO WORK® INSTITUTE INC.

Pfeiffer
A Wiley Imprint
www.pfeiffer.com

Published by Pfeiffer
An Imprint of Wiley
989 Market Street, San Francisco, CA 94103-1741
www.pfeiffer.com

The following phrases/names used throughout the manuscript are trademarked or copyrighted by the Great Place to Work® Institute:

Great Place to Work® Institute
Great Place to Work® Model©
Trust Index© Survey
Culture Audit©
Best People Practices© Data Base
FORTUNE 100 Best Companies to Work For® Annual List

To contact Pfeiffer directly call our Customer Care Department within the U.S. at 800-274-4434, outside the U.S. at 317-572-3985, fax 317-572-4002, or visit www.pfeiffer.com.

Pfeiffer also publishes its books in a variety of electronic formats. Some content that appears in print may not be available in electronic books.

ISBN: 978-0-470-59833-7

Acquiring Editor: Holly J. Allen
Director of Development: Kathleen Dolan Davies
Production Editor: Dawn Kilgore
Editor: Rebecca Taff
Designer: izles design
Manufacturing Supervisor: Becky Morgan

Printed in the United States of America

Printing 10 9 8 7 6 5 4 3 2

GREAT WORKPLACE LEADERSHIP ASSESSMENT

Instructions: Below are several statements that correspond to the likelihood that your employees experience a great place to work in your department. As you respond to the statements, consider the work group for which you have direct responsibility and influence. Note that sometimes this will be different than the group of people who formally report to you on an organizational chart.

FOR EACH OF THE FOLLOWING STATEMENTS, DETERMINE THE FREQUENCY WITH WHICH YOU DEMONSTRATE THE BEHAVIOR OR PRACTICE. USE THE FOLLOWING SCALE:

1 = I never or rarely engage in this behavior

2 = I sometimes engage in this behavior

3 = I often or almost always engage in this behavior

The results of this assessment will be most useful to you if you are thoughtful and honest about your responses. Also, be sure to respond based on how you actually behave, not on how you intend to behave.

☐ **1.** I allow people to take time off when they need to.

☐ **2.** I am myself at work; I express my beliefs and concerns openly while doing what is best for the organization and the team.

☐ **3.** I make sure people are aware of how to appeal decisions made by their leaders.

☐ **4.** I actively welcome and respond to questions.

☐ **5.** I work to alleviate the collective stress of my work group, be it due to personal, time management, or financial causes.

☐ **6.** I role model a sense of pride for the organization and its products.

☐ **7.** I know what people in my work group enjoy doing outside of work.

1 = I never or rarely engage in this behavior

2 = I sometimes engage in this behavior

3 = I often or almost always engage in this behavior

☐ **8.** I have an understanding of the benefits the organization offers, and I help people to understand how they can best take advantage of them.

☐ **9.** I recognize people when they do a good job, regardless of their position or tenure in my work group.

☐ **10.** When people are promoted in my department, I communicate to others their qualifications for the new role.

☐ **11.** I encourage and reward cooperation in my work group.

☐ **12.** I make decisions in a timely way.

☐ **13.** I am aware of the abilities and capacity of people who work in my department/work group and ensure that they have challenging assignments and a manageable workload.

☐ **14.** I take opportunities to bring fun to our work.

☐ **15.** I ask that my team members gather input from people, in our department and others, before making decisions.

☐ **16.** I communicate about the distribution of profits made by the organization.

☐ **17.** I disentangle myself from political situations when I find myself involved.

☐ **18.** I role model the behavior expected of people at our organization.

☐ **19.** I go out of my way to make new hires feel welcome.

1 = I never or rarely engage in this behavior

2 = I sometimes engage in this behavior

3 = I often or almost always engage in this behavior

20. I frequently tell people how their unique skills and talents benefit the team and the organization.

21. I recognize that mistakes are a necessary part of doing business.

22. My actions are consistent with the values of the organization and my own public statements.

23. I help my team to understand how our work together makes a difference.

24. I role model a healthy work/life balance.

25. I foster a warm and supportive group spirit in my team.

26. I encourage people to be a part of community events sponsored by the organization.

27. I freely share information with people to help them do their work.

28. I show respect to people in other departments throughout the organization.

29. I encourage people to celebrate special events.

30. I create opportunities for us to decide together on the best course of action.

31. I make sure people are involved in the decisions I make that affect them.

32. I openly share my vision of the future with people and suggest ways that we may reach our goals together.

1 = I never or rarely engage in this behavior

2 = I sometimes engage in this behavior

3 = I often or almost always engage in this behavior

---

33. I tell people when I think they've done a good job or expended extra effort on a task.

34. I coordinate or support activities (such as team lunches) to help employees transferring to my department feel welcome.

35. I coordinate or support activities (such as team lunches) to help new hires feel welcome.

36. I give people opportunities and treat people with respect regardless of their personal characteristics (e.g., race, age, gender, sexual orientation).

37. I ensure that my team gets information about how our organization impacts the community outside of our operations.

38. I treat people with respect no matter their position in my work group or the organization.

39. I take care not to spread rumors.

40. I let people in my department do their jobs without micromanaging.

41. I help people connect their day-to-day responsibilities with the larger purpose of the organization.

42. I help people understand how the work they do makes a difference.

43. I make sure people have the resources they need to do their jobs well.

44. I try to avoid giving any employees preferential treatment.

1 = I never or rarely engage in this behavior

2 = I sometimes engage in this behavior

3 = I often or almost always engage in this behavior

---

45. I encourage people to be themselves and to respect the individuality of others.

46. I regularly share information with people about our industry, operations, and financials.

47. I hold people accountable for the quality of their work.

48. I work to ensure fair pay for the people in my work group.

49. I encourage people to balance their work and their personal lives.

50. I seek input, suggestions, and ideas from my team.

51. I ensure that people understand the factors influencing their pay.

52. I follow through on my promises, large and small.

53. I work hard to ensure that what I do aligns with what I say.

54. I enable people to obtain the training and development they need for their career success.

55. I know the career "next steps" for each person I supervise, and I create opportunities for them to have relevant experience to meet their career goals.

56. I give people a clear idea of what is expected of them.

57. I celebrate team accomplishments.

Instructions: Transfer your scores for each item in the Corresponding Statements column onto the appropriate line. Then sum the items for each sub-dimension, and divide by the number in the Average column. Finally, check the box (strength, area of potential, area of opportunity) that corresponds to your score for each sub-dimension.

DIMENSION	SUB-DIMENSION	CORRESPONDING STATEMENTS	AVERAGE	STRENGTH (✔ IF OVER 2.8)	AREA OF POTENTIAL (✔ IF 1.9 TO 2.8)	AREA OF OPPORTUNITY (✔ IF BELOW 1.9)
CREDIBILITY	**Two-Way Communication**	4 _____ 27 _____ 46 _____ 56 _____ Total _____	/4=	◯	◯	◯
	Competence	12 _____ 13 _____ 32 _____ 40 _____ 47 _____ Total _____	/5=	◯	◯	◯
	Reliability	18 _____ 22 _____ 52 _____ 53 _____ Total _____	/4=	◯	◯	◯

DIMENSION	SUB-DIMENSION	CORRESPONDING STATEMENTS	AVERAGE	STRENGTH (✔ IF OVER 2.8)	AREA OF POTENTIAL (✔ IF 1.9 TO 2.8)	AREA OF OPPORTUNITY (✔ IF BELOW 1.9)
RESPECT	**Support**	21 _____ 33 _____ 43 _____ 54 _____ 55 _____ Total _____	/5=	☐	☐	☐
	Collaboration	15 _____ 30 _____ 31 _____ 50 _____ Total _____	/4=	☐	☐	☐
	Caring	1 _____ 5 _____ 7 _____ 8 _____ 24 _____ 49 _____ Total _____	/6=	☐	☐	☐
FAIRNESS	**Equity**	9 _____ 16 _____ 38 _____ 48 _____ 51 _____ Total _____	/5=	☐	☐	☐
	Impartiality	10 _____ 17 _____ 39 _____ 44 _____ Total _____	/4=	☐	☐	☐
	Justice	3 _____ 36 _____ Total _____	/2=	☐	☐	☐

DIMENSION	SUB-DIMENSION	CORRESPONDING STATEMENTS	AVERAGE	STRENGTH (✔ IF OVER 2.8)	AREA OF POTENTIAL (✔ IF 1.9 TO 2.8)	AREA OF OPPORTUNITY (✔ IF BELOW 1.9)
PRIDE	**Individual Pride**	20 _____ 41 _____ 42 _____ Total _____	/3 =	☐	☐	☐
	Team Pride	23 _____ 57 _____ Total _____	/2 =	☐	☐	☐
	Organizational Pride	6 _____ 26 _____ 37 _____ Total _____	/3 =	☐	☐	☐
CAMARADERIE	**Intimacy**	2 _____ 29 _____ 45 _____ Total _____	/3 =	☐	☐	☐
	Hospitality	14 _____ 19 _____ 34 _____ 35 _____ Total _____	/4 =	☐	☐	☐
	Community	11 _____ 25 _____ 28 _____ Total _____	/3 =	☐	☐	☐

ANALYSIS AND INTERPRETATION

Most self-assessments suggest that you zero in on opportunity areas and create action plans based on them. While this does provide the sort of systematic review of data that can be helpful in your personal development, it's not the whole story. There is something to learn from your strengths, areas of potential, and areas of opportunity. We present the following guide below for analysis and interpretation.

STRENGTHS

If your score for a given sub-dimension is 2.8 or above, it can be considered an area of *strength*. Chances are that people in your work group are experiencing a great workplace with regard to this sub-dimension.

REFLECTION QUESTIONS: While considering your strengths, ask yourself the following questions in order to learn even more from them.

- Why do these behaviors come naturally to me? Is there some underlying personal characteristic that drives these behaviors? How might I use that characteristic to address areas of opportunity?

- Is there some characteristic of the work environment that makes these behaviors easier for me? Are there other ways I can capitalize on these environmental characteristics?

- Do people in my work group appreciate these behaviors? What, specifically, does it help them do or experience?

NEXT STEPS: As you analyze your areas of potential and areas of opportunity, consider how your strengths may be helpful to you.

■ Is there a way to build upon my strengths in order to improve in other areas?

■ Are there personal, environmental, or work group characteristics that I can incorporate in my action plans?

AREAS OF POTENTIAL

If your score for a given sub-dimension ranges from 1.9 to 2.8, we'd consider this an area of **potential**. In essence, people in your work group are experiencing the behaviors sometimes, but not often or always. In great workplaces, we see a great deal of consistency in the experience of behavior on the part of leaders. Your action steps here may be as simple as increasing the frequency of the behavior, but it may help to investigate further before doing so.

REFLECTION QUESTIONS: While considering your areas of potential, ask yourself the following questions in order to learn even more from them.

- When I do exhibit these behaviors, what underlying personal characteristics might I be relying upon? Likewise, is there some personal characteristic that I don't possess, but would help me do this more often?

— - — - — - — - — - — - — - — - — - — - — - — - —

— - — - — - — - — - — - — - — - — - — - — - — - —

— - — - — - — - — - — - — - — - — - — - — - — - —

— - — - — - — - — - — - — - — - — - — - — - — - —

- When I do exhibit these behaviors, what is going on in the work environment? Are there ways to make that set of circumstances happen more often? When I do not exhibit these behaviors, what is going on in the work environment? Are there ways to remove those obstacles?

— - — - — - — - — - — - — - — - — - — - — - — - —

— - — - — - — - — - — - — - — - — - — - — - — - —

— - — - — - — - — - — - — - — - — - — - — - — - —

— - — - — - — - — - — - — - — - — - — - — - — - —

- What is the impact on my work group when I inconsistently exhibit these behaviors? Is it merely that they don't benefit from my doing it more often? Or does my "half-way" approach produce confusion and mixed messages?

— - — - — - — - — - — - — - — - — - — - — - — - —

— - — - — - — - — - — - — - — - — - — - — - — - —

— - — - — - — - — - — - — - — - — - — - — - — - —

— - — - — - — - — - — - — - — - — - — - — - — - —

NEXT STEPS: Determine whether there are action steps in these areas that will improve the experience of people in your work group.

- Is it possible for me to rely on my personal strengths to increase the frequency of these behaviors?

- Is it possible to change the work environment to enable more of this behavior? Are there obstacles I can remove?

- How might I use the experience of people in my work group to help me determine how to turn this area of potential into a strength?

AREAS OF OPPORTUNITY

If your score for a given sub-dimension is below 1.9, we'd consider this an area of **opportunity**. In essence, people in your work group are not experiencing the behaviors with any consistency. While a knee-jerk reaction may be to focus all of your attention on these areas, we find that there is often a reason they are not occurring naturally. Investigating them first allows you to determine the root cause of the area of opportunity.

REFLECTION QUESTIONS: While considering your areas of opportunity, ask yourself the following questions in order to learn even more from them.

- Is there some personal characteristic that I don't possess, but that would help me do this more often? Is that personal characteristic rewarded in my organization? Is training readily available?

_____

_____

_____

_____

_____

_____

- What is going on in the work environment that may prevent me from exhibiting these behaviors? Are there ways to remove those obstacles?

_____

_____

_____

_____

_____

_____

- What is the impact on my work group when I do not exhibit these behaviors? Are their needs being satisfied elsewhere? What are the consequences of that?

_____

_____

_____

_____

_____

NEXT STEPS: Determine whether there are action steps in these areas that will improve the experience of people in your work group with regard to these behaviors.

- Is it possible for me to develop personal characteristics that may increase the frequency of these behaviors? Is it possible to rely on strengths I already have, but have not applied to this situation?

  _____

  _____

  _____

  _____

  _____

  _____

  _____

- Is it possible to change the work environment to better enable this behavior? Are there obstacles I can remove?

  _____

  _____

  _____

  _____

  _____

  _____

  _____

- How might I use the experience of people in my work group to help me determine how to turn this area of opportunity into a strength?

  _____

  _____

  _____

  _____

  _____

  _____

  _____

Discover more at **www.pfeiffer.com**

Pfeiffer®
An Imprint of
WILEY

ISBN 978-0-470-59833-7
90000

9 780470 598337

That Patchwork Place®

1st ed.

THE ULTIMATE BOOK OF

Quilt Labels

MARGO J. CLABO

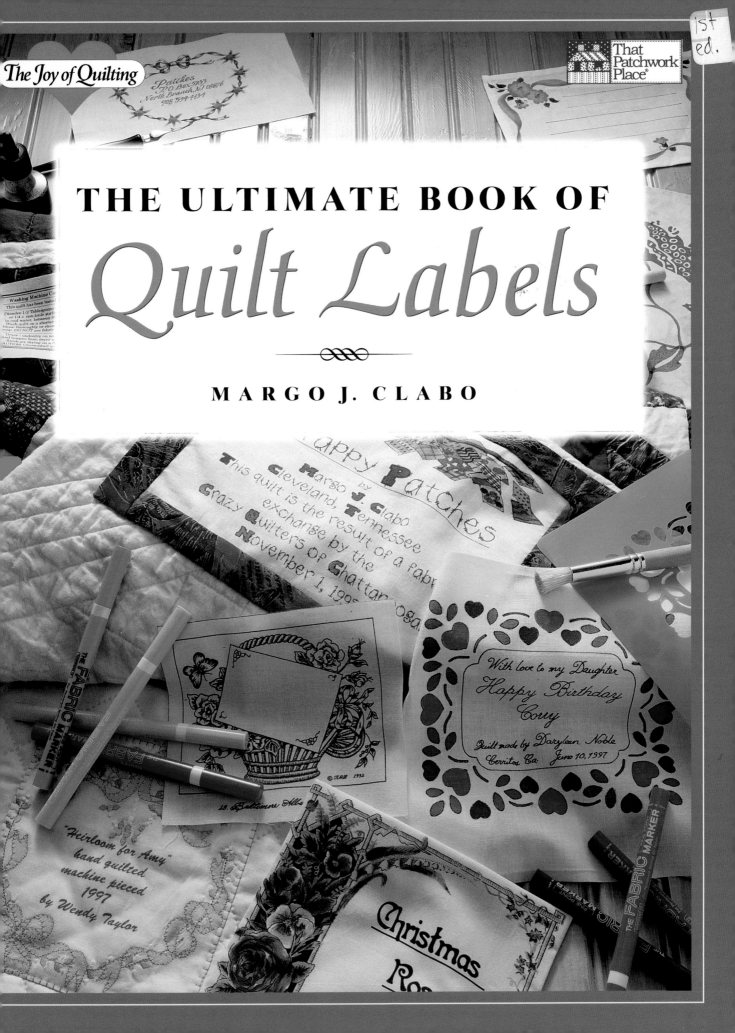